Three's A Crowd

Trios that can be performed with any other combination of instruments from Book A.

Piano accompaniment

plus guitar chords arranged by James Power.

CHESTER MUSIC

London/New York/Paris/Sydney/Copenhagen/Berlin/Madrid/Tokyo

Exclusive distributors:
Chester Music
(a division of Music Sales Limited)
8/9 Frith Street, London W1D 3JB, England.

Music Sales Corporation
257 Park Avenue South, New York, NY 10010,
United States of America.

Music Sales Pty Limited
120 Rothschild Avenue, Rosebery, NSW 2018, Australia.

Order No. PM221765R
ISBN 0-7119-9392-0
This book © Copyright 2002 Chester Music.

Instruments featured on the cover provided by Macari's Musical Instruments, London.
Models provided by Truly Scrumptious and Norrie Carr.
Photography by George Taylor.
Cover design by Chloë Alexander.
Printed in the United Kingdom.

Your Guarantee of Quality:
As publishers, we strive to produce every book to the highest commercial standards.
The music has been freshly engraved and the book has been carefully designed to
minimise awkward page turns and to make playing from it a real pleasure.
Particular care has been given to specifying acid-free, neutral-sized paper made from
pulps which have not been elemental chlorine bleached. This pulp is from farmed
sustainable forests and was produced with special regard for the environment.
Throughout, the printing and binding have been planned to ensure a sturdy, attractive
publication which should give years of enjoyment.
If your copy fails to meet our high standards, please inform us and we will gladly replace
it or offer a refund.

Music Sales' complete catalogue describes thousands of titles and is available in
full colour sections by subject, direct from Music Sales Limited.
Please state your areas of interest and send a cheque/postal order for £1.50 for postage
to: Music Sales Limited, Newmarket Road, Bury St. Edmunds, Suffolk IP33 3YB.

www.musicsales.com

Contents

Lavender Blue

Traditional

Little Brown Jug

Traditional

Twinkle Twinkle Little Star

Traditional

Clementine

Traditional

Moderato

Sur le Pont d'Avignon

French Traditional

Allegretto

London Bridge Is Falling Down

Traditional

8

Old MacDonald

Traditional

Kum Ba Yah

Traditional

Go Down Moses

Spiritual

Looby Loo

Traditional

Au Clair de la Lune

French Traditional

Skip To My Lou

Traditional

This Old Man

Traditional

The Run Around

James Power

Big Rock Candy Mountain

Traditional

16

Dance Of The Hours

A.Ponchielli

Delicato

Aaron's Beard

James Power

Yankee Doodle

Traditional

Mairi's Wedding

Irish Traditional

20

Li'l Liza Jane

Traditional

Quartermaster's Stores

Traditional

When Johnny Comes Marching Home

Traditional

Yellow Bird

Traditional

24

O Susanna

Traditional

Early One Morning

Traditional

How's Your Father

James Power

Boston Belles

Traditional

A Marcato

Fine

B

D.C. al fine

Snap

James Blackford

29

Can Can

J. Offenbach

30

D.% al Coda

The Highland Lassie

James Power